FEAR

THE DRIVING FORCE

KEVIN HICKS

FEAR: THE DRIVING FORCE

Typesetting: Kenya Gould

Cover Design: Kenya Gould (www.designsbykenya.com)

ISBN: 978-1-7365656-0-5

Printed in USA

FEAR: THE DRIVING FORCE

CONTENTS

INTRODUCTION

For God hath not given us the spirit of fear. If God didn't give it, how did I get it? Where did it come from? I can feel fear and I can sense it. It speaks to me in a quiet voice, can you hear it?

After years of athletic competition, which include high school, college, professional, and post-professional, I've discovered one thing: fear was always present. Fear was always changing its shape, always presenting itself in new ways that I could not have imagined. It was like a sneaky predator, it watched from a distance and pounced when I least expected it. At the end of a long athletic career, I can look back and see how fear moved and how it made attempts to cripple me from my future.

By definition, fear can be described as terror, panic, distress, agitation, and a whole host of other unpleasant emotions induced by perceived danger. Every morning an individual rises up to live their life, fear exists. It is an ever-present emotion that many people don't acknowledge nor deal with. Fear can push you, hinder you, strangle you, confuse you, and more. Fear is an emotion that has great influence on your decisions, behavior, and standard of living. Fear is controlling and manipulative, it will make you rethink everything you knew.

This book is written for the athlete, businessperson, and every living individual who strives to better their life. As you read this book, please take the opportunity to look into your personal life and see where fear is hiding and how it is affecting you. It is my hope that as you identify fear in your life you can address it and overcome it.

CHAPTER ONE
THE FEAR TO TRY

One of the easiest identifiable behaviors of fear is the fear to try. As an experiment, ask a close friend or family member to try something new. Chances are their first response will be "no" or "I've never done that before." This response can stem from a lack of confidence or from not wanting to embarrass themselves. The number of reasons one can use to decline trying is infinite. What's important to note is that fear is behind these decisions, preventing people from taking the necessary steps to make their lives better.

In our everyday lives, we strive to create, perform, and take on various activities. These activities can take the form of starting a business, starting a non-profit, running for government or local office, and the list goes on. Each of these activities requires an individual to take some initial steps to make their dreams a reality. Some steps are easier than others. For example, filling out necessary paperwork or spending money on your idea is easy in principle because of the small amount of effort or resources required. Some steps in the process may be a little harder, though, such as standing in front of a crowd asking for their vote, asking people to support your business, or even showing up on the athletic playing field.

As a young athlete developing my skills, I've learned that the fear of trying appears at every stage of development. Most notably, there is the fear of trying a new sport or activity, trying a different approach to an activity, or listening to a coach or mentor who challenges your standard way of doing things. One reason for this fear is personal comfort. The default human behavior is to do what is comfortable, and when we are asked to do something new, we compare it against previous known actions and activities.

But what is actually known? Our previous experiences provide an outlook on how to start and how to finish an activity. These experiences allow us to reflect on expected outcomes. Good or bad, we accept these outcomes when we make our decisions. However, when we take steps to get outside of our comfort zones, we begin introducing new variables to the equation. These variables all lead to one question: "what if?"

"What if" is a two-word question that will overshadow any decision and cause doubt. What if I don't win? What if I don't finish strong? What if I can't make it to the finish line? "What if" is the single most used mental phrase that cripples an individual from moving forward. Basketball players ask themselves these questions every time they make a pass, shoot, or jump for a rebound. And the mental answers to these questions may be: someone might block the shot, step in front of the pass, out-rebound me, or foul. Utilizing American Football as an example, a quarterback may ask, "what if I throw an interception?" In track, it could be, "what if I take the lead a lap or two early?" As an athlete, you find yourself saying what if constantly. However, it's important to identify where it's coming from, what is causing it, and how to overcome it.

Businessmen and women should note an athlete's experiences, struggles, and emotions and learn to use them to their advantage. The world of business is not different from athletics. Everyone is in business to make money, but the nature of business is to compete against others. Businesses compete against local, regional, national, and global entities. Some businesses have great leadership; this is called coaching. Some have great facilities by way of financing. Some experience a great deal of success, which comes through heart and determination. A small subset of businesses has none of these. Each business should be able to identify one athlete that reflects their current position in the world. For example, a world leader in business may compare themselves to the world's greatest athletes, while a business startup may compare themselves to a rookie in a sports league. The world leader has all the accolades and accomplishments, while the rookie has lots of ambition and drive. In this manner, businesses can uniquely evaluate themselves to identify what needs to be improved or how to go about it.

Once a company identifies its position and role, it needs to compete in its respective economy—local, regional, or national. A business may need to hire a CEO or a coach to compete adequately in the changing times. If they need to expand, they will need financing, and if they aren't earning business, a little bit of effort and self-determination can improve their situation. In each scenario, the required action must be taken. While making these decisions, corporations will become acquainted with their list of "what ifs." What if we pick the wrong CEO, what if we cannot get financing, what if we make an additional effort and cannot make additional sales? These are all valid questions and concerns for any business.

Ultimately, the fear of trying causes a knee-jerk reaction. Whenever you have an opportunity to try something new, fear will appear and cause you to retreat instead of going after your purpose.

CHAPTER TWO
THE FEAR OF TAKING SECOND

Competition, by its very nature, can be a scary thing. It requires action, effort, and perseverance. To engage in competition recognizes that you are striving to reach a goal. The process of competition is like going on a journey. There will be other competitors attempting to reach the same goal. Some will arrive before you, some after you, and some, possibly, at the same time as you. Some people will steal your methods and techniques to improve their own. They will copy your plans, listen to your conversations, and infiltrate your team huddles. They will use your public communications and marketing efforts for inspiration and use that inspiration to beat you, destroy you, or even to work with you. The beauty of competition is that it provides everyone a chance to perform, stand on the stage, and earn their fifteen minutes of fame. Everyone is competing for the championship. Whether you arrive first, second, third, or last, someone else will always be looking at things from their own perspective to get what you have. Your job, your position, and your ranking are to be protected at all costs.

Take a moment to look back over your life. Can you acknowledge how competition has existed at every stage of life? For example, as children, we compete in spelling bees, academics, and board games. As adults, we compete against each other as employees, employers, and general marketplace participants. Everyone has something that they are working on or working towards. We can agree that all we want to do is win, no matter what. The difference between each competitor is where they stand when the lights go out.

Since we desire to win in all forms of competition in all aspects of our life, our default behavior is to be afraid to lose. No one wants to take second place. Therefore, we must address the "what if" of not winning. What if I don't win the championship, land the job, cannot have children, or gain acceptance to my favorite college or organization? The list of winning activities is endless, personal, and unique to each person. If we examine more extreme circumstances, parents will compete for the last bag of pampers and milk at the supermarket just so that their child will not go without. Once that parent makes it to their home, they will brag about how they overcame a fierce battle in the grocery store to come away with the last bag of pampers.

However, once we have achieved our first-place trophy, what then? What's next? To avoid taking second, athletes will spend extra time in the gym, while employees work extra hours just to show that they are better than everyone else. This is our default behavior, knowing there is always someone on our tail trying to steal our trophy.

When interviewing the world's greatest athletes, they will confirm their desire to avoid taking second place. They will go to great lengths to avoid it at all costs. If you ask them why they don't want to take second place or how does second place make them feel, they will be hard-pressed to give you a direct answer, but any answer they give will be deeply rooted in fear of not arriving on top. No one is entitled to first place; therefore, everyone must work, study, and demand their position.

Some will say they trained their whole life to achieve greatness, and they never took a day off. But why? Is it because of the fear? Fear of not being the best. Quite simply, it is the fear of being second.

The journey to the top for businessmen and women can be more lethal. Companies can lie to their customers and cheat their vendors to earn the title as number one. Everyone is competing to be the best business globally, therefore, exaggerating earnings and inflating sales are tactics used to secure a victory. Multinational companies brag about being at the top of any magazine list, quote billboards, bloggers, vloggers, and anything else that provides them exposure, to convince the world they are the best.

The pressure to achieve and overachieve is rooted in fear. It's right before our eyes, and we can't see it, don't acknowledge it, and dismiss it completely. However, on Monday morning, everyone will open their morning paper to research what their competitors have done over the weekend to sustain their competitive edge. The main thought in our minds is, "if I can figure out what someone else did, what they are about to do, or what I should do, then I can win." But if I take a second, somehow, I have not worked hard enough, researched enough, or done everything possible to succeed.

CHAPTER THREE
THE FEAR OF WINNING

Once upon a time, you were the greatest, feared by everyone in the land, never willing to accept second place. Now you are skipping practice, arriving late to appointments, not giving your best in social interactions. Smile and nod, they say, they call it doing just enough to get by, in some circles. Your company is still making money, bills are getting paid, but the drive to overcome and overachieve is not the same. Complacency. I thought you were going to go, do, and achieve. That's right, you forgot, you were too busy, or you simply decided not to take action.

The fear of winning acknowledges that you are actually in the race. However, you did not put forth your best effort to beat the competition. You show up to the fight but won't show out. The world wants to see your greatness, but you won't display your unique skills, moves, or talents. The fight is happening in the competition field; however, you are stuck fighting a real and personal battle, stuck in your thoughts, opinions, and emotions.

Your internal battle has taken away from your efforts to achieve the goals and dreams you desire. It has placed weight on you and has given you multiple reasons regarding why your goals are unachievable.

You've got to empty the bucket and give it all you've got.

The lights are shinning, the camera is focused on you, but it's so easy to tuck your tail and ride this one out. That's not all; the media won't ask any questions. If you get second place, you are allowed to walk on by without a comment. Winning requires an explanation. Some people simply don't want to explain themselves. To win means you have to field the tough questions and tell the world about your success. The world will want to know, "how did you do it?" "Why did you do it?" "Can you do it again the next time?" And, "can you share your secrets so we can do it too?" These questions create self-reflection. Even considering self-inspection can create the perfect conditions to instill fear and prevent you from moving forward.

Can you allow yourself to be the first to cross the line? Can your business be the first to implement a new solution to fix an industry-wide problem? Are you capable of answering the questions, being in the spotlight, or handling the attention from such a feat? This is what separates winners from losers. In your imagination, can you see yourself on the front page of a major publication?

How do you determine your feelings and emotions toward winning? Practice! We're talking about practice! Before game day, you have the opportunity to work on your weaknesses and strengths. One tip is to take some alone time. During this time, it helps to meditate, stretch, and rest. Listen to your thoughts and emotions. They will speak loud and clear. They may say, "I don't feel like it today," "I can't do it," or "it's too hard." You've got to see yourself doing it mentally. If you can't push yourself to do it alone or at practice, how can you expect to perform during the real game? Gameday is a reflection of your preparation, which requires practice. While it will be nice to flip the switch on game day, certain things come only from practice, such as conditioning, strength, your game plan, and your attitude.

To be the best, you have to compete and win against the best. If competing against the best in your division is intimidating, how can you compete regionally or globally? Therefore, your attitude has to be stronger and more resilient than the best. Suppose you are afraid to win, then why start your business or step into the athletic competition? At the very least, make every attempt to do your best or set your goals that define your version of winning.

CHAPTER FOUR
THE FEAR OF CHANGING TACTICS

Sometimes, your competition knows how to get the best of you. When you go right, they go left. When you go high, they go low. A strategy is key to any performance. You need to know what you will do if a new situation presents itself. All too often, competitors fall into easily identifiable patterns. In sports like football and basketball, athletes study game tapes of their competitors. They so do to identify the tendencies of a team or player in certain circumstances.

As an individual, you also have tendencies and if you are watched long enough, your actions can be predicted. Tendencies are not a bad thing if they work for you. For example, consider your favorite athlete; can you easily identify their favorite moves? If you can, chances are they use these repeatedly as an effective tool to win. But what if your tendencies do not work for you? What do you do?

The first step is to identify which behaviors create your bad tendencies. Once these are understood, the next step is to figure out what stimuli can be introduced to retrain your old behavior patterns into better, successful ones. When you retrain bad behaviors, it makes you a better competitor because you can react, counter, and move forward in the fight. Can you identify patterns in your behavior that someone else can easily identify? What are your tendencies that, if studied, can be used to defeat you or outsmart you? It's important to understand these about yourself; then, you can be one step ahead of your competition.

Once you have identified your bad tendencies, now it's time to decide to do something different. For example, a basketball player who always goes right will make the change to go left. Initially, these changes may be uncomfortable. Even after much practice, you may find yourself repeating old habits. The thought of changing bad habits may be more difficult than the actual action, though. Bad tendencies create dependencies, and this is where our fears lie. "If I introduce change, it may cause me to be a better person, and I'm happy where I'm at."

Changing tactics is critical to a business. For example, a life insurance company may be using direct mail methods to acquire clients. However, so does everyone else. As a result, customers may have created behaviors like throwing the mail away before opening it. A new approach may be to use social media marketing to reach a targeted demographic. A business may be cautious of this type of approach because it's new, innovative, or out of the ordinary. Just because it's different does not mean it can't be beneficial. Strange behaviors can generate unorthodox responses, creating an edge to remove the fear and take the step.

CHAPTER FIVE
FEAR OF PEOPLE'S OPINIONS

Words. People's opinions are real things. They have weight. Some of them even have merit. They are a force to be reckoned with. Opinions can make you happy, sad, or mad. Businesses may change their entire business models based on them. Athletes endure them constantly. If they're not spoken, they're written, and if they're not written, they're shared publicly through social platforms. Public Relations firms specialize in this. A journalist can't live without them. Regardless of your stance on it, at some point, you'll fear them. We all do.

Opinions can cause an individual to lose their job. It doesn't matter if it's yours or theirs. Opinions can cause you to be alienated by businesses. It can stop you from getting a promotion or receiving a raise. Opinions can play a big part in your emotions. They can cause you to behave out of character. Maybe you were offended, or you took something personally. Letting your emotions get the best of you can have unintended consequences. Those consequences can affect your performance, health, and mental state.

Opinions come with expectations, which can push you to further your goals or push you away from them. An expectation is an extension of an opinion. These expectations can travel with you wherever you go.

For example, any athlete ranked in the top ten of their respective sport is accompanied by the public's expectations. Whenever a top ten American football receiver does not make a catch, the fans will say, "he's supposed to make that catch because..." As you can see, the world will place expectations on you, based on what you have shown them.

The pressure to win, meet expectations, and validate opinions is so deeply ingrained in our society that men and women have caused harm to themselves. Have you ever noticed a similar trend in your life? Can you identify one area where you made a decision that was not in your best interests because of the opinions of someone else? The truth is we all have.

How do you identify that a person's, an organization's, or society's opinion is causing stress or strain on you? In each category, we must identify where an opinion or expectation is acting as a weight on you. Then identify what you want to do about it. Do you want to change your way of thinking or approach in this area? Do you want to continue living according to these expectations because "that is just the way life is?" Whichever direction you decide to take, at least you can now identify them. In this manner, you are one step closer to understanding the fear behind your decisions.

But how do we overcome it? Do you ignore it? Listen to it? The truth is, you must listen to yourself, you own desires and make a plan of attack to do what you want to do. There will always be opinions, good and bad. You will have to face them no matter what you do, might as well do it your way and face opinions later.

As a business owner, the opinions of the people involved in your business are more critical. Investors, shareholders, partners, financiers, and customers all have opinions on how you should conduct business. They all equally share and force upon your business their ideas of what you should and should not be doing. That force has caused Fortune 500 companies to do an about-face on policies to remain in favor and good graces. To be pulled in so many directions at once makes everything a difficult balancing act. Imagine a tug of war, where the rope spread in eight directions. For starters, it would be difficult for one opinion to win. Still, more importantly, the company, which is at the center point, will spend most of its time traveling back and forth between the eight points, never finding a solid footing as it is continuously yanked back into the opposite direction. Therefore, businesses will do their best to remain neutral out of fear of being cancelled, boycotted, or facing other adverse actions.

CHAPTER SIX
FEAR OF FAILURE

Can you identify moments in your life where you have said to yourself "I'm going to fail," "no one else has been successful at this," or "every time someone makes an effort, they lose?" These are a few of the many ways we express the fear of failure.

Have you ever asked yourself "what if I fail?" Why did you ask yourself this? This question is a common one and it must be quickly tackled quickly with a solution; otherwise, you will remain on the battlefield with questions instead of actions. Solutions may include self-encouragement or support from other people.

Consider all the ideas you have had in your lifetime. While each idea might have been a good one or easy to accomplish, can you identify which step in the process created the most fear and caused you not to start? Was it the effort it would take to get your ideas going? Did it require you to come face to face with a fact that was out of your control? For example, many people work toward buying a house, but one step in that process is getting their credit in good standing to qualify. In some senses, previous mistakes may make it impossible to qualify or achieve success in the future. Or maybe you didn't start because you would be the first in your family to ever achieve such a goal? Does being the first mean it's impossible?

A potential business owner may elect not to purchase additional equipment or hire new employees because they are unsure if the additional help will bring higher profits. Additionally, a company may elect to start a new project but only implement half of its requirements because they do not know how the market will accept or adapt to it. For this reason, many businesses sit on the sidelines, waiting for the perfect opportunity. In reality, it is the world that is waiting for them to overcome their fear and bring their product to market.

A common behavior with the fear of failure is the lack of action. Each day you have a desire to make progress and take the steps to achieve your goal, but the thought of each outcome causes you to turn back and wait. As you gain daily inspiration, you imagine each stumbling block that could impede your progress or knock you down. Focusing on the stumbling blocks creates worry, which is an undeniable force of stagnation. Remove the negative thoughts, focus on the next step ahead, and make your dreams a reality.

CHAPTER SEVEN
FEAR OF SUCCESS

When one considers a goal, they must first see themselves attaining it. Goals are often lofty thoughts that can take a significant amount of years, struggle, and determination to achieve. In the beginning, some goals appear so out of reach that they may seem impossible or unattainable. For example, a young athlete may have aspirations of winning an NBA championship. While their journey may start with high school sports, then college, then the NBA, their actual goal of winning a championship is the pinnacle of success.

To share these goals and ideas publicly can be met with negativity. "You will never make it.", "No one from the east side has ever gone that far." As a dreamer, it is easy to aspire to the highest levels of greatness only to have your closest supporters deflate your dreams. Be careful to not accept their reality as truth. Your goals and dreams are not tied to the people around you now. In fact, once you have arrived, those people won't be there any way.

Your inner circle can fear for your success. They do not want you to take a chance because you may fail, or more terrifyingly, you may succeed. They fear your success because it causes them to self-inspect and ask themselves why they haven't achieved greatness. It is easier for them to crush your dreams than to see you succeed. By doing so, it makes them feel better. They will brag about how good you were and how you had a shot to make it big and will silently be glad that you didn't make it. Can you identify any friends or family members who encouraged you to dismiss your dreams? Or are you the type of person who silently wishes for their friends to fail?

The second type of success you might fear is your own. You, too, can look at your goals and decide it's too much. You may have natural gifts and talents that can take you around the world, but for whatever reason, you decide that it's not what you want. But you keep talking about it and dreaming about it daily, weekly, monthly. No one is holding you back—in fact, you may not even have told anyone, possibly because of a "what if." What if I succeed? The fear is so strong, and you won't give yourself a chance to attain it.

And some of us, as we are making actual progress toward our goals, once we are too close to the mountaintop, we find a reason to jump off the ledge. This is called self-sabotage. There is no reason to fear the thing you work toward every day. Grab your dreams and take hold of them. Sometimes you do not get a second chance.

CHAPTER EIGHT
FEAR OF CONSEQUENCES

Consequences are a real and tangible result that waits to make its appearance after you've made a decision and have taken action. Consequences can be positive or negative. However, the thought of consequences can stop a person in their tracks from making a decision.

In order to understand consequences, we need to identify questions or actions that lead to consequences that may make you fearful. Sample questions include "what if I take a new job?" "What if I go back to school?" "What if I start a new business?" The thought of consequences—the loss or gain of something important—creates an examination of reality. In most cases, that something is security. Am I giving up a good job to go into a worse situation? If I start the business, I won't have money to support myself and I will be all alone. I may have to work extra hours, having less time for family and friends. Every decision you contemplate is important and can jeopardize the stability and security of your known reality, in exchange for the illusion of something that could or could not happen. While it is true that some consequences are known because they are written into law or presented as a prize, they shouldn't not stop you from taking positive action.

Think about a time when you considered an important decision. It could be about a major purchase, an incredible business opportunity, or helping a family member. While the action or gesture was well intended, the what ifs surrounding the purchase, cosigning, or helping family posed major challenges if things hadn't worked out as expected. The fears that follow up as a result are self-imposed. These fears create worry, which is rooted in the thoughts of the worst-case scenarios. Considering the worst-case scenario first is a default pattern that causes us to make a safe decision, but it also hinders us from attaining what we want in life.

In business, one common fear is the threat of legal attack. Legal consequences create a genuine fear, so much so that businesses will threaten each other with action because they all share the same inherent fear. Even the largest corporations with the largest number of attorneys will make business decisions based on the consequences of their actions. Examples of business consequences include the risk of government questioning, customer boycotts, or negative public relations. Legal consequences create significant security challenges that can affect a business' bank account and the way it does business. This is why corporations consider settlements in place of litigation. In some cases, a corporation may acknowledge unethical behavior and create a change in business practice to prevent fines or other legal consequences.

As it relates to customers, businesses will consider the thoughts, feelings, and emotions of their customer base before making a decision. They will make decisions guided by the fear of what a customer may do in retaliation. They will allocate funding to hire experts to guide them in areas that they are weak. Businesses will implement processes to avoid consequences at all costs. Businesses' overall fear is the unknown, therefore, each decision has an area of uncertainty that must be protected against.

CHAPTER NINE
COURAGE

The ability to tackle fears head-on is called courage. Courage, by definition, means to do something that frightens an individual. The first ingredient of courage is fear, which is present in all areas of life. The second ingredient is to take action where the fear exists. One cannot have courage unless they are afraid. With this understanding, fear is a good thing that should be embraced because it provides an opportunity to utilize courage by standing up to things that make us fearful.

In order to use courage, we must self-evaluate all the "What ifs" we create in our head that we are afraid of. By creating this list, we can make a plan of action to overcome these fears and begin to establish a database of times we used courage to overcome fear. "I remember," is the phrase that captures each opportunity fear was present, but courage overcame it. Can you remember a time where you were once fearful? Can you remember what you did to overcome your original fear? If you are still fearful, would you take the same action to challenge your fear again or would you do something different.

Courage does not prescribe one action, but leaves the door open to any thought or action to overcome fear. Courage can take advice from others who have been in a similar situation. It can use trusted techniques used within the community, or it can invent new actions and methods once believed to be impossible. Courage techniques can be found from reading and trial and error.

Courage will accept help from a roommate, a friend, or a stranger on the street. It could be as simple as "hold my hand," "watch me to make sure I don't fall," or even "help me." Therefore, you don't have to do it alone. For fears that are too much for you, ask for help. Fears that cripple you do not necessarily cripple everyone else as well. Remember that you are not alone in your battle if you share it, but no one knows you're fighting if you keep it in your head.

APPENDIX A

Make a list of the "What ifs" you are afraid of below. Label them with each area they apply to (e.g. fear of winning, fear of consequences).

Identify techniques you can use to overcome your fear. Add names of individuals you may know who can help you overcome areas that are too difficult for you.

Now that you have documented your fears, the steps you need to take to overcome them, and individuals who can help you, it's time to implement the plan. Utilizing your plan, the best way to overcome fear is to take it step by step. Don't be overly concerned with the outcome. Make an initial effort and let each additional step take you to your goal. Plan ahead, understand what's coming next, and be okay with your decisions. On your journey, you may find additional levels of fear. These should also be documented, to help you understand where you came from and where you are going. In the end, fear is only an emotion. It is something that you can feel, something that you can sense. But it is not something that belongs to you because you have courage as your tool to overcome, defeat, and be rid of fear.

APPENDIX B

FEARS – CHEAT SHEET	
Fear to Try:	Purposely not making any effort.
Fear of Taking Second:	Purposely overachieving to avoid losing.
Fear of Winning:	Purposely making an effort to avoid winning.
Fear of Changing Tactics:	Avoiding changing approach to remain comfortable.
Fear of People's Opinions:	Avoiding making a decision because of people's opinions.
Fear of Failure:	Avoiding trying that will lead to unexpected outcomes.
Fear of Success:	Avoiding attaining goals.
Fear of Consequences:	Avoiding action because of an expected outcome.

ABOUT THE AUTHOR

Kevin was born in Miami, FL. He attended Miami Central High School, where he earned State Championships in both Cross Country (XC) and Track. As a collegiate athlete, he won the NCAA and USA National Championships. He is a former professional athlete and member of Team USA's World Championship Track Team.

His earliest memories of track were full of desire and anticipation of reaching the highest levels of athletics. To reach those levels, he trained as hard as his body would allow on a daily basis. He challenged the status quo by pushing himself beyond his fears, the expectations of others, and the reality of his inner circle. Through his experience, he is able to share a unique and detailed point of view for the everyday man, woman, and child.

www.ingramcontent.com/pod-product-compliance
Lightning Source LLC
Chambersburg PA
CBHW060046050426
42448CB00012B/3128